Colo—State—Pen: 18456

A Dark Miscellany

W.K. Stratton

LITERARY PRESS
LAMAR UNIVERSITY

ISBN: 978-1-942956-55-6
Library of Congress Control Number: 2018946067

Lamar University Literary Press
Beaumont, Texas

Also by W.K Stratton

Dreaming Sam Peckinpah

Ranchero Ford/ Dying in Red Dirt Country

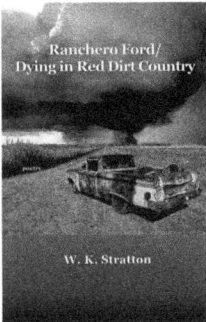

Recent Poetry from Lamar University Literary Press

Bobby Aldridge, *An Affair of the Stilled Heart*
Michael Baldwin, *Lone Star Heart, Poems of a Life in Texas*
Charles Behlen, *Failing Heaven*
David Bowles, *Flower, Song, Dance: Aztec and Mayan Poetry*
Jerry Bradley, *Crownfeathers and Effigies*
Jerry Bradley and Ulf Kirchdorfer, editors, *The Great American Wise Ass Poetry Anthology*
Matthew Brennan, *One Life*
Mark Busby, *Through Our Times*
Paul Christensen, *The Jack of Diamonds is a Hard Card to Play*
Stan Crawford, *Resisting Gravity*
Chip Dameron, *Waiting for an Etcher*
Glover Davis, *My Cap of Darkness*
William Virgil Davis, *The Bones Poems*
Jeffrey DeLotto, *Voices Writ in Sand*
Chris Ellery, *Elder Tree*
Mimi Ferebee, *Wildfires and Atmospheric Memories*
Larry Griffin, *Cedar Plums*
Ken Hada, *Margaritas and Redfish*
Lynn Hoggard, *Motherland: Stories and Poems of Louisiana*
Michael Jennings, *An Affair of the Stilled Heart*
Ulf Kirchdorfer, *Chewing Green Leaves*
Laozi, *Daodejing*, tr. By David Breeden, Steven Schroeder, and Wally Swist
Janet McCann, *The Crone at the Casino*
Jim McGarrah, *The Truth About Mangoes*
J. Pittman McGehee, *Extraordinary in the Ordinary*
Laurence Musgrove, *Local Bird*
Godspower Oboido, *Wandering Feet of Pebbled Shores*
Dave Oliphant, *The Pilgrimage*
Carol Coffee Reposa, *Underground Musicians*
Jan Seale, *The Parkinson Poems*
Steven Schroeder, *the moon, not the finger, pointing*
Carol Smallwood, *Water, Earth, Air, Fire, and Picket Fences*
Glen Sorestad, *Hazards of Eden*
W.K. Stratton, *Ranchero Ford/ Dying in Red Dirt Country*
Loretta Diane Walker, *Desert Light*
Wally Swist, *Invocation*
Jonas Zdanys, *Red Stones*
Jonas Zdanys, *Three White Horses*
For information on these and other Lamar University Literary Press books go to
www.Lamar.edu/literarypress

For Jerry Craven

CONTENTS

"That is the truth as it has come down to me," said Old Lodge Skins. "And the same thing happened many times thereafter, whenever the white people appeared. They do not like each other, and sooner or later one will kill the next, and usually not in battle, the way our people do to prove themselves brave and to enjoy the courageous deaths of our enemies and to die on a good day, but rather by shooting in the back or stretching the neck or by infecting one another with the coughing sickness and sores and making people lose their heads with whiskey."

Thomas Berger, *Little Big Man*

NOTE

I never knew anything about my paternal grandfather, Don Carlos Stratton, Sr., until I was well into my forties. Even then he was an obscure figure, at best, for several more years. Then, when public records and newspaper archives became available in abundance online, I learned a great deal about him, though the picture remained incomplete. He was born in the early 1870s and was around sixty when he fathered my father. He died a decade before I was born. He was not a good man. He was a criminal, an embezzler and a conman, who avoided getting caught and punished until he was sixty-five years old. Then he went to prison in Colorado. Worse, he treated women abysmally throughout his life. He also abandoned his family. My father, Don Carlos Stratton, Jr., was not a good man either. I know he was married at least six times. He didn't always bother with divorce when he determined it was time to end a marriage. I also know that he was a wife-beater. And he abandoned me and at least one other child. I never had any contact with him until he was a box of ashes that I retrieved from Oregon (no one else wanted it). He inherited a lot of bad traits from his father, my grandfather. He also cultivated some of his own.

One day I sat down to write a poem about my grandfather, to capture what I knew factually as well as I what I'd imagined. It wound up taking months to finish "COLO—STATE—PEN: 18456," a poem running almost forty pages. I would call it an epic but there was nothing heroic about my grandfather. I would call it a mock epic, but there's nothing funny about it. It's about a bad man behaving badly.

It and the other pieces in this collection were written at a time when men behaving badly—in particular, behaving badly toward women—reached a crisis point in America. I know a woman who is a psychological counselor. She deals with issues involving sex and relationships, specifically what is known (and often dismissed) in some quarters as sex addiction and love addiction. She told me that research indicates that there could be a strong genetic component to bad men behaving badly. Like father, like son, in other words—the apple never falling far from the tree. What did that portend about me, then? How far was my apple from the far reaches of my father's and my grandfather's trees? As I speculated about that, I turned to my imagination once more. I began writing poems and prose scrapbook fiction entries, some built around real incidents and real people I knew (and know), some about an alter-ego of myself, others completely made up. Only a very few of these are about the "real me"—the chili poem is "real," for instance. Some are a blend. I wrote "Morir Soñando" while I was in El Paso, and I had been listening to the music of the late, great Valerio Longoria while driving around the city, but the rest of the poem is purely made up. Well, let's say mostly. I won't go into detail. But you should consider these as persona pieces.

COLO—STATE—PEN: 18456 is volume three of a work I now call the *Dreaming Sam Peckinpah Quintet*. Volume one was *Dreaming Sam Peckinpah*; volume two, *Ranchero Ford/Dying in Red Dirt Country*. Sam Peckinpah was one of the great artists of my lifetime, an absolute master of film. He was also a man who had an infected soul. In this, he was not unlike the male personae in these pieces. In his case, the disease was exceptionally bad. He explored symptoms and root causes in all his films, but especially so in *Bring Me the Head of Alfredo Garcia*, that difficult and dark and haunting masterpiece.

These are such difficult compositions that I made next to no effort to publish them in periodicals. But special thanks go to Kat Georges and Peter Carlaftes, who have included me regularly in their splendid *Maintenant* collections of Dada art and poetry. It is a true honor to see my work in those pages, including some of the pieces in this volume.

Also, I owe Thomas Zigal and Steven L. Davis a debt of thanks, both for their friendship and support as well as for their help with this book.

As much as anyone else in recent years, Jerry Craven showed faith in me as a poet. He edited and published those first two volumes of the quintet; he also designed their magnificent covers. For that reason and more, I warmly dedicate *COLO—STATE—PEN: 18456* to him.

WKS

HOW BILLY BECAME BILLY

I.

My mother named me Billy. Not William. Not Bill. Billy. I guess she talked to my father about it, but maybe not. They weren't together when I started breathing.

Why did she pick that name? I can't say.

When I was a little boy, I manufactured a reason:

She took a look at me and determined I was the second coming of Billy the Kid. That was my fantasy. I'm certain it couldn't have happened that way. But that was my fantasy.

II.

That's why I've always been proud to be called Billy. And I suppose that's why I've had this near-lifelong fixation on Billy the Kid, Billito, el mal hombre from the Pecos Valley. We know everything about him. We know nothing about him. We know where he is buried—unless he is buried somewhere else. We know where his mother is buried—unless she is buried somewhere else.

His mother, Catherine McCarty. What a piece of work she was. Maybe she immigrated to New York City during the Great Potato Famine and scraped for a life in the blue catastrophe of that metropolis. Was McCarty her given name? One she adopted to hide from herself and everyone she knew? The last name of a husband or at least of a man who fathered one or both of her sons? No one can know. Did she work the cobbled streets of Corlear's Hook? Is that how she contracted consumption? Again, we don't know. And more: Did she ever keep time with a man named Bonney? Did he provide the seed for one or both of her sons? Or was that name snagged from a Pecos Valley hail storm and sewn to Billito's chest? No answers. Did she bear those boys a stone's throw from the Bowery? Probably. Or were they born in Indiana or Missouri? Or somewhere else? Probably not, but there's no way to deny locales positively. Okay, I'll say this with certainty: Neither the Kid nor his brother was born in the Sandwich Islands.

III.

Catherine sliced through the Midwest, a woman stronger than most men, a razor for a business mind, stone eyes that abided no shit. But she also spoke with a lilt and had a laugh no one could forget, that no one ever wanted to forget. She made herself known in Wichita. She shared her bed with a man to whom she was not married, a man named Antrim. He may or may not have been half-worthless. He dreamed of mines and the easy life. She worked her Irish ass hard, cooking, cleaning, boarding men more worthless than her bedmate. She made the money while Antrim dreamed. Everyone who counted in Wichita during its muddy cowtown splendor knew her and respected her. Even if she was a strumpet. Her sons, her boarders, her next-door neighbors would hear her cry out during sex at two o'clock in the morning. Always that time of day, and she was always loud. By three-thirty in the morning, she was out and about with lantern, milking her cows.

IV.

Legend has it that Antrim possessed a strip of meat like a young pony's. He had few other virtues. And may not have possessed that one.

V.

Catherine invested well in Wichita. But a doctor and a priest both told her she would die soon if she remained there. Her lungs could not withstand the humidity and dust and heat. The priest told her hell awaited her unless she—a baptized Catholic, a confessed Catholic—forsook Antrim and her lustful ways. She never spoke to a priest again. But she listened to the doctor.

She subscribed to Presbyterianism thereafter.

VI.

She sold out and the four of them set out for the Rocky Mountains, leaving Wichita behind, Colorado in mind.

They traveled in a wagon train pulled by oxen teams. There on plains flat and hard as a skillet bottom, Kansas surrendering to eastern Colorado, the boy Henry McCarty—as Billy the Kid was called then—began to come into his own. He saw a buffalo herd that stretched endlessly away, like a muddy lake. He saw Cheyenne raiders for the first time. They swooped in on painted horses, attempting to steal anything they could. They got away with horses and a couple of calves. An old man traveling with the train dropped one of the Cheyennes. The old man fired a Colt M1861 Navy revolver, a cap-and-ball gun that was louder than a thunderclap. Henry's ears still rang when everyone gathered around the Cheyenne's body.

Should we scalp him? someone asked.

Fuck, no, the old man said. It was the first time Henry heard anyone say fuck in front of a woman. We don't walk in their dirt.

What do we do?

The old man stepped up to the body, straddled it, unbuttoned his pants—right there in front of the women and children and everyone—took out his wrinkled tiny penis and proceeded to piss on the dead Cheyenne. He was an old man, as I said, so it took him forever to empty his bladder. But he finally finished. As he buttoned up, he said, now we'll leave his bony ass for the wolves and coyotes to fight over.

No, someone said, those Indians will come back for him. They'll take him with them, to bury him in the way savages think is proper.

The old man pulled out his Colt and fired off three rounds, one into each of the Indian's eyes, the last one into the Indian's groin. I know them superstitions they carry with them, he said. They see him like this, they'll ride away in a hurry. Best get this train rolling.

That night, Henry hardly slept. He had visions of a big Cheyenne with no eyes and no pecker pursuing him under the fires of the prairie.

That night, he spoke to himself about right and wrong.

The next morning, he told Catherine he wanted to be called Billy from now on. She slapped him to the ground.

VII.

He dreamed of riding.

17

PART I

BLOOD POISON

COLO—STATE—PEN: 18456

I.

Lower these ruby-lidded haints through night
Mosquito gauze. Hawks hit the river flat.

A child hickory beaten draws revenge and love.
His father snores with stepchildren and flames.

The river is gray and chocolate, flows its name
Apart from the adjacent state with no sound

Save tugs and barges.

Indiana shore, coal nostril, and water disease—
Republican and Presbyterian—

The black-eyed Strattons are known for fists
After whiskey plugs and stoneware nightmares.

Dream onward, boy bruised, burning eyes dispersed—
Dream onward, slipping clay, typhoid vapors.

II.

So, across the Ohio River, mile wide
Maybe, twenty-foot-deep in lead sludge,

An uncle and his new woman await.
The city smells of distilled corn and yeast.

Descendant of King Solomon Stratton,
Kentucky corralling family reach and stain,

He discerns his stake.

He is below what he steals and conceals.
His hand unfolds in blossoms dim as hair.

He understands only his eyelid shade.
Whiskey and log chinks welcome his jangle—

Burgoo ladled with boiled potatoes
And a cracked schooner of Stratton brown.

III.

We keep our coloreds in line on this side,
The uncle speaks to him. *They make fine grooms.*

The new woman wears a yellow house dress,
Naked beneath the folds, nipples mud-colored,

Black nest junction atop her sour milk thighs.
She breathes his eyes recording each sway and dip.

Don Carlos Stratton.

Your daddy called you after old man Buell?
The fib-spouting goat of Pittsburg Landing?

It's a name, the boy says, *we all have one.*
He sees freckles crumbling from her smooth neck

And rolling down her breasts. She laughs two times.
He knows she will convert his sheets before dawn.

IV.

First time, Indiana side, was a whore
Who deposited herself as Noreen.

Wind-draft cabin stinking cat shit, her lair—
Two hundred pounds of woman, no matter,

He claimed his three-dollar rut, baptized, stout,
In this faith of sweat and carved vessels:

He'll worship harlots.

Noreen lit her corn cob. *You should fly west,*
She said, hard-peckered boy like you can build

Monuments to himself there. Everything
Here Is buried. Her breast is a gunny sack

Collapsed on his twelve-year-old elbow.
Kentucky now, but the West, yes, the West. . .

V.

He lifted those dollars from his daddy,
That first moist prong—Noreen, divination.

The Ohio pushed westward, as did trains.
He studied and dreamed and tested mud.

Break-even labor at stables and saloons,
Nothing more than a fool's occupation.

You'll need money.

Women and Kentucky whiskey—dollars.
Barber talc and hand-cut suits—dollars.

Hustling on the platform, eyeing hiked skirts—
You'll need money—jewels unguarded.

A man wearing galluses and bowtie
Approaches, sawing, *This is not your way, son. . .*

VI.

You require education, not schooling.
You require bluff of hand, not parchment.

You spit-shine your mind, it will pay off.
You paint your collar, you know coin jingle.

You learn every man falls to sparkle.
You learn every man pockets his eyesight:

Something for nothing.

You cannot cheat an honest man. True words.
Thank God no rightly honest men stroll this earth.

Thank God everyone aches for the big score:
Money stuffed sacks for a five-spot wager.

Sashay this permanent night alley, friend,
Don't be everybody's fool—here you win.

VII.

Money rolls two directions: banks, railroads.
Too many eyes vaulted at banks—embrace trains.

Keep a pistol, keep it well-oiled and straight.
Never flash it unless you mean to shoot.

But you never want people thinking you are
A man who totes cold steel and cartridges.

Don't sport on horses.

A dozen pen strokes in your ledger
Fetches more cash than igniting bank vaults—

—Neat Jim Treet, galluses and talc teaching—
Practice the handwriting of twenty men.

And Don Carlos: No, that name will not fly,
Can't have people thinking you're Mexican.

VIII.

So just Don C. now, barbershop dapper
Under Neat Jim's ice visage, working trains,

Rehearsing a dozen men's handwriting:
Sign names upside down, draw them, don't scribble,

Pay mindful heed to spaces twixt letters,
Crowded lines lead to the hangman's loop. . .

Ink blues his fingers.

Bring that bottle over here, Green Street whores
And sanctified bourbon brown, bent-knee rewards

For first insurance vouchers claimed in full,
Sunday Presbyterian prayers of thanks.

Never repent for what the world owes you—
You are the wildcat's yowl, the wind, the sleet.

IX.

Insurance fraud: that is his Baptism.
Mr. R.D. Loudermilk transporting

Three hundred seventeen core samples,
Value: four hundred eighty-three dollars,

Claim filed with Ohio Palisades Loss
& Casualty of Cincinnati,

R.D. Loudermilk

Drawn fine by Don Carlos Stratton,
Fingers fluid as turpentine and whiskey.

Draft arrives in seven weeks, forge the name
One more time, sign it over to Jim Treet.

Neat Jim works his La Grange first bank magic.
Your piece, young man, is a grand one-fifty.

X.

And it is whiskey, whores, and a new suit,
Fifty dollars secreted under boards,

The year, 1888, the West calls—
Louisville shudders beneath its own weight.

The West, the West, the West—he inhales it.
He prays it, he sings it, he sublimes it:

Buffalo gals out.

He totes nickel digests within his vest.
He recites Billy the Kid in saloons.

He stands before mirror, dreams Cody hair
And whiskers, buckskin, fringe, turquoise visions.

Sixteen years old, and big country abides.
Shuffle off old Louisville, goodbye town. . .

XI.

...and THE WEST
Wild Bill and Buffalo Bill
Pawnee Bill and another Bill—

March 7, 1888, our year,
William Temple Hornaday
credits himself with a kill,

Old Bull, largest buffalo known
in that time/taxidermy
then mounted with a spike bull,

two cows, a yearling, a suckling
in glass/come see!
THE WEST!

Smithsonian crowds gawking—

two years before
Geronimo surrender
Skeleton Canyon

One Who Yawns
a prisoner now
no purpose left/I had lost it all

vanquished Apache faces
posed along Southern Pacific tracks
outside Uvalde, Texas,

Nueces River
en route Fort Sam Houston,
THE WEST!

cavalry troopers watching—

and three years before that
Patrick Floyd Jarvis Garrett
murderer of Joe Bricoe

one-time hog farmer
husband of two Mexican sisters
hate-filled kitchen fights

no eres un hombre, eres una cabra
green eyes untrusted
unlocks Billy the Kid's chest

to New Mexico night air
¡Billito, es asesinado!
THE WEST!

butcher knife tumbling—

and land rushes, gold rushes,
Indians naked, skull mountains,
Sharps rifle, .50-90 caliber, mister

Chinese all but slaves
laying virgin track
don't show your yellow ass in town

Pendleton, Oregon, Chinese underground
step down for cheap whores and opium
painted over for white eyes

or so you hear, who knows?
story trumps ledger ink
THE WEST!

every cliché rooting—

big river, big forest
big desert, Great Plains
mountain high in crumble

dying buffalo, crawling Indians
towns built by slackjaws
goddamn, what a place!

trade a wagon of pelts
for an unused daughter
of a lost Missouri plowman

pack a bag, change your name
and set off for life renewed
THE WEST!

emptied pockets filling—

towns with names like Portland,
Denver, Boise, Missoula,
Albuquerque, Las Vegas

oh, so much for a man to carry
shaky deal in Prescott, maybe,
quick train ride to Cheyenne

set them up, do it again
remold it every time
deposit wives and children in arrears

carry a Bible, exhale a pistol
Big Six Wheel, Bola Tangkas
THE WEST!

eastern river fading—

XII.

He stares out at that zinc river water.
Old men hack coal smoke and fired green wood.

He tongues his whiskey cup and ponders whores,
New ones, just up from New Orleans,

Maybe even a black woman or two,
Skin like toasted bread with honeyed butter,

Evening breast nuzzle.

Men the color of his morning coffee
Hit banjo, guitar, jug, and tub bass—

He hears it through the open window.
He wishes he knew the harmonica.

All he can do is hum and scratch his pen
On ledger books, foot tap time as years pass.

XIII.

Any fool who followed the Republican newspapers knew it was War coming. I heard it in the dram shop. I heard it from the Presbyterian pulpit. I heard it from the colored porters. It was war and it was past time. I hated the Spanish because I hid a few in my own woodpile, my eyes dark as coal from the number nine split, my bootblack hair. Don Carlos.

And Neat Jim Treet—well, that man smooth as talcum lost twenty-seven pounds in six weeks and told me he knew of Pinkertons prying around the freight dock. His face had swallowed his eyes. He viewed me through creases. My good man, war can save the afflicted. Can you ride? Yes. Can you march? Maybe. Save your hide and sign the line when the time comes.

I cared less about Carlos M. Céspedes and the Grito de Yara or José Julián Martí y Pérez or any such nonsense. I knew only that they found Neat Jim two and a half miles up the Salt River, back of his head blown away by a shotgun, his hands and feet cut off, those swallowed eyes and staring creases remaining on a face that somebody wanted recognized.

That was in April, wildflowers in the ditches in north Kentucky. The next day Congress resolved to sail troops to Cuba. By then I had a Canadian wife with a stepchild I didn't cotton to, an idiot girl. I told the woman I wanted that girl gone. Fix it. After supper, I looked through the dining room lace and saw two men wearing dusters and derbies on the walkway.

I enlisted in the Army the next morning, April 21, 1898. I was twenty-six.

XIV.

Dearest Mary Gordon, i trust in god
and jesus that you have a better day
than me because nothing can be worse
than in a camp with morons and thieves

sheriffs and such never come
after a man in uniform during a war
you will be safe in our house
we play some 7-Up here
when we can get a deck
there aren't too many.

XV.

I dreamt of Cuban beauties with breasts bare, melting themselves into me in endless surf. I dreamt of kicking the old Spanish soldiers onto their boats and sending them home and walking in hero parades down cobblestones of Havana. I dreamt of cheers and gaming halls, just a short boat ride from Florida.

The goddamned Army.

They sent me to Puerto Rico.

XVI.

He has trouble pronouncing Ponce
In the local manner. He loathes the sun.
He sweats in his cot, a sergeant for sure
But he knows each platooned boy hates him.
No matter, he will not be with them long.
Mosquitos bite worse than in Louisville,
Somehow piercing the netting overhead.
One morning he could not rise from his cot.

His joints ache, he shivers without control.
In two days his face and eyes burn yellow
And he throws up black blood and bile.
The Puerto Rican boys who carry him
Mutter *vomito negro*.

They nail him with dying men.

XVII.

and now I lay me   *each breath a storm*
in a long low Ponce room   *Spanish everywhere*
sweat drop from an arched ceiling   *puke pail*
I can't focus   *you must try to eat*   *vomiting again*
Puerto Ricans happy for coins carry dead men
on folding stretchers   *I have a medal*
pinned to a piss-stained pillow   *I am broken*
please, eat   *comer*   *lips dry as rock*
bury me in Kentucky, but not goddamned Indiana
ever hear of W.S. Stratton?   *he's my cousin*
hit the motherlode on Pike's Peak   *southside*
got the hell away from the Ohio River   *smart*
he's the one   *made it West*   *rich*
gave Crazy Bob Womack $5000 in cash   *hated*
to see a prospector down on his luck   *devil rich*
              not dying of Satan's disease here
in goddamned Puerto Rico   *he went West*
he went West   *my cousin*

XVIII.

and   when fever dies   way, away
they feed him beef broth and bread he doesn't
know   they give him   coffee
        and makings, Bull Durham   tremble
of hands and soul   yet a smoke is good
broth and bread, broth and bread   then real food
and finally he's on a transport ship   rope cot
rocking with waves and breezes   New Orleans
port awaiting, port forgiving   he lands
then runs and runs

                                dreaming half-truths
in boarding houses   in shanty room rentals
                broken and creased
and then   because there is nothing else
he surrenders to the Army   court martial
busted, sergeant no more   Private Stratton
less than honorable discharge, Stratton   yes sir
but it's only ink scratches   in a ledger
no one will read
no one will know
a war hero
back in
Louisville

XIX.

River: gray, brown, sometimes green, unending
And Louisville in red, white, blue blunting

For returning soldiers, and Stratton marches
In azure wool among them. He next becomes

A Freemason, then a Rotarian,
A solid citizen, the lord of fraud,

But betrays the wait.

And so those men return, same as before.
Outside his house in rain, derbies lustrous.

He's heard of brine-soaked hands and steel knuckles,
Palmed pistols, gouged eyes, man up the river

Demands his piece—remember Neat Jim Treet!
Hands atremble, he smooths paper then writes:

XX.

woman, do not disregard this
pack all you can that will fit
woman, take this sober
we are leaving on the 11:36
i have it all planned
we will call Portland our home now
it is a fine place
i'm told
ask no questions

XXI.

Leaving a place forever is sliced cake
And a hot cup of coffee.
Never see the muddy Ohio again
And that's fine, daddy, that's fine.

XXII.

fragment from a newspaper article—

Portland Police officers last night arrested Don Carlos Stratton, railroad clerk, for insurance fraud and embezzlement. Stratton, who police believe has been in Portland for about six weeks, will be held, pending bond, until the grand jury convenes next month. At present he is in the City Jail, with no bond set. It is believed that he is married and the father of a child. Police say Stratton, aged 30, processed three separate—

XXIII.

fragment from a newspaper article—

. . .for which he was arrested. Stratton, believed to be aged 32, failed to appear for arraignment ten days after his wife posted bond and he was released. He is not considered dangerous. However, officers believe he was a flight risk, and the City's depots received notice to be on the lookout for him. He is described as a tall man with eyes black as a new moon. His hair likewise is black. Though his middle name is Carlos and his features are dark, it is unknown if—

XXIV.

They slip town on a southbound train.
Save the cash for the man in L.A.,
The man who knows Brazil,
The man who tells him he'll never learn
        Portuguese, but—
The man who knows Brazil is out of reach,
The man who knows re-creation
Of a soul bent and sallow.

They settle in Rio— beauties on the beach
Beauties in the brothels
Beauties who never speak a word he
        understands
He makes some money.
Mary Gordon demands snow.

XXV.

Eyes like the morning star/cheek like a rose/Laura was a pretty girl/
God Almighty knows/weep all ye little rains/
wail winds wail/all a-long a-long a-long/the Colorado Trail/

And a steamer to L.A., then the fast train to Denver:
It occurs to him in Arizona Territory what they want—
Haul your ass out of here, don't trail back.
It's the apt prescription for him.

He hugs himself in his freedom.
His wife beside him refuses his eyes.

XXVI.

Poison blood wipes Denver streets.
You speak of him, and he is I,
I am you, no difference.

Poison blood as he moves business to
       business,
Tipping every ledger, gilding each
       lead pencil point,
Ink smears on his sharp shirt cuffs
       no matter
Money pressed deep into each pocket.
Don C. Stratton—Presbyterian, Republican,
       family man,
Buddy of old Ben Stapleton and more,
20th century ragtime joy.

Drink the heavy glass, work a scam,
Two different whores a week,
Wife retreated in light poor rooms,
Never blessing him
       no matter
Poison blood flows as he travels
From director to director
Today and tomorrow
Forever rejoined.

Decades slide.

XXVII.

The War To End All Wars came and went. Carlos G. signed up and fought, never thought he had such in him. Mary G. sat alone and cried. He returned and erupted law school, Denver University, damned good student. A genius for patents. Made him a fortune. Went off to Mexico to be a writer, of all goddamned things. I never got a taste for jazz myself. When the chills descended I drifted straight to the Soldiers and Sailors Home, Homelake, and shivered until the disease swallowed itself. Carlos G. came back, slid a wife he claimed bore another man's child, then went to Los Angeles. Mary G. died and two hundred people crowded First Avenue Presbyterian to see her hauled to a muddy grave. The harlot from New York arrived two years later. I liked what I saw of cow hands projected on a sheet in a half-finished building on Fifth Avenue back in '12. But as movies and moviehouses grew larger, I felt smaller. We had Mexicans aplenty in Denver but I never ran with one who liked jazz. Mercy those people could toil away at anything. Never knew a white man to do such.

XXVIII.

The days close in, the nights fade.
He follows himself to the harlot's
      abode
And sinks in her groove as her daughter
Sleeps on the nightstand next to
      the bed.
He steals more to give her more.
She opens herself to give him more.
Lawyer's wife from Brooklyn fair,
Run amuck to the Rockies, fleeing
Her Winthrop Fleet cabinetry,
The grand Puritan name of Lockwood.
He becomes a Shriner, red fez proud,
And rocks with her near to every night.
She swells with another man's child,
      already with three of her own,
No matter. The child takes his last name
At birth, Peggy Stratton, and he maintains:
Two years later another child,
This one his own:

Don C. Stratton Jr.
My father, his son.

XXIX.

Dollars.
Dollars dollars dollars:
He taps the till, he dresses in black,
He makes the deals, holds back the cash.
They climb to a larger house, marriage license signed.
They maid splurge and hire a lawn man, never mind the age,
Soup kitchens in Larimer Square, dead flophouse curtains,
The rage of nothing, the slide of stale bread—none matters
In the house with Mexican cleaners, flash of calf thrilling him,
When the harlot isn't looking. An automobile, clothes and
Toys for the boy who wears a cowboy hat and begs rodeo
With his first words. Never mind whores now, he's married
To the best, who allows him to subsist while she sways
In flourish, Anna Lockwood Newell, who calls
Herself Joan for reasons unknown, sometimes
Joanna. Sometimes, she says, I want to own
A carnival, wouldn't that be exciting?
He inks ledgers for mines and oilfields
And real estate. Nothing interests him,
Not any more, except a shave
And haircut and nice dusting
Of talc.

They arrest him in 1935.
He is sixty-three years old.
Dollars.

XXX.

They say a Texas woman showed up at my cousin's office,
Winfield Scott Stratton, that is,
And demanded money for a child
She claimed he spawned.

She fled Colorado and disappeared in a town
Called White Settlement,
No dollars exchanged.

I called on him once myself, back in '01.
A snub-nose ruddy boy in an office said
He would kill me himself
If I didn't leave. Pronto.

I never saw my cousin's face.
I have no idea what I hoped to get.

They say he attempted a Brown Palace room
With the wife of his attorney.
Mr. Stratton—we can't permit that sort of thing.
He nodded, bought the hotel with a personal check,
Fired the night clerk,
Checked himself and his lady into a room.
Midas of Cripple Creek—
Why did I aspire it?

XXXI.

No men in fez hats attend him.
Mayor Ben Stapleton ignores pleas.
None of his mushroom buddies arrive.
He is done, he is done.
Never mind his age, sixty-three really?
He is dispatched to Cañon City steel,
Where he labors in the fiber rooms,
Lungs filling with thread and lint:
COLO—STATE—PEN: 18456,
His serial number on dapper mugshot,
A tonsorial man among shootists
And knife wielders: *he is done. . .*
His new wife and namesake son
Reduced to Larimer Square flophouse,
No mind. . .
When parole comes he flees to California
Where the first-born Carlos Gordon
Has made himself rich in Pasadena sunshine.

The old man never saw my father again. . .

XXXII.

He proclaims schemes and things
But Carlos Gordon locks him
In a room abutting Stratton Lane,
South Pasadena—*don't let him
Run loose.* Idiocy and irony descend quickly.
Pre-dawn on Stratton Lane,
Carlos Gordon has the back door open:
Two men foxtrot inside and carry out
The old man.

*Wadsworth Hospital,
Sawtelle, West L.A.*

And Rio and Louisville and Ponce
All merge as one in a brain
Dissolving. He pisses his pants
And drools his porridge,
Eventually tied to the iron
Of a bed frame—
Neat Jim Treet, galluses and talc teaching—
It means nothing to attendants.
I can write like twenty men!
They backhand the old convict into silence.
I've known more women than Douglas Fairbanks!
Years of this, then
Cancer and dementia
Dissolve him for good,
October 25, 1946.
Back east, the Ohio
Rolls uncaring.

XXXIII.

Slide him into a hole of L.A. soil,
A fine and proper graveyard.
Carlos Gordon has his mother
Dug up from Denver dirt
And replanted here in SoCal sunshine.
All very nice, all very nice.
Respectable Strattons—
Carlos Gordon in an L.A. high-rise office,
Children clean at South Pasadena High.
All very nice.
All very nice.

Let no one speak of anything in the past.
Nothing at all.

PART II

MÚSICA OSCURA

TWO SAMS IN THE HURRICANE

My mind fled to Parras del Fuente in black dawn. Sam Peckinpah strolled there, wheat jeans bloodied by hemorrhoids and despair. He lied to his script supervisor and himself. And so it always had to be. Flies trailed him. Desire trailed him. He stumbled on his own failures. He was an artist with a pistol tucked in his belt.

Later I ignored Texas police warnings and drove out into what was left of the hurricane. Lawn chairs and trash cans tripped across my asphalt. I brought no rain gear. As always, I turned into the cemetery. A tree branch smashed the earth ahead of my car. I hiked through wind and rain to Sam Bass's grave. Sam Bass—a total fuck up until it came time to die. Then he demonstrated what a gut-shot saint should be. Townspeople spread him out on the floor of a simple room. Someone placed a school book on his chest to watch it rise and recede. When the book slipped to the floor, they knew it was time to commit him to the caliche.

Mostly it was former slaves who gathered around the grave that day. They sang him to whatever lies next, as real human beings do. I stand there now. Storm shredded leaves paste my face.

STEEL GUITAR
(after Grover Lewis)

JG O'Rafferty | Herb Steiner | Buddy Emmons |
      Sneaky Pete | Tom Brumley | Norm Hamlet |
      Lloyd Green | Don Helms | Al Perkins |
Paul Franklin | Jerry Byrd | Speedy West |

Pete Drake | John Hughey | Jerry Brightman |
      Jimmy Day | Bud Issacs | Rusty Young |
      Leon McAuliffe | Sol Hoopii | Noel Boggs |
Herb Remington | Shot Jackson | Alvino Rey |

Joseph Kekuku | Buddy Cage | Jay Dee Maness |
      Red Rhodes | Curly Chalker / Ben Keith |
      Don Jernigan | Chubby Howard | Hal Rugg |
Kayton Roberts | Freddie Tavares | Gabby Pahinui |

Cindy Cashdollar | Greg Leisz | Stu Basore |
      Joe Kaipo | Peewee Whitewing | Cousin Jody |
      Bob White | Sonny Garrish | Buck Reid |
Bashful Brother Oswald | Don Warden | Ernie Ball |

Hank DeVito | Buddy Charleton | Neil Flanz |
      Jay MacDonald | Doug Jernigan | Lucky Oceans |
      Lloyd Maines | Jeff Newman | Joaquin Murphey |
Little Roy Wiggins | Eddie Alkire | Dick Kaihue McIntire |

David Kelii | Bobby Garrett | Billy Robinson |
      DeWitt Scott | Johnny Sibert | Barney Isaacs |
      Jimmie Crawford | Tom Morrell | Herby Wallace |
Fuzzy Owen | Dusty Rhodes | Jimmy Grabowske |

Walter Haynes | Bobby Black | Leonard Zinn |
      Maurice Anderson | Roy Ayres | Julian Tharpe |
      Bud Carter | Ron Elliott | Dicky Overbey |
Terry Bethel | Lynn Owsley | Jim Vest |

Ralph Mooney
Moon

PUNK AND MERLE HAGGARD

Tonight I hear Television's *Marquee Moon*
Storm inside my skull.
She watches television in another room,
Insipid Sandra Bullock refuge
I can't understand.

When my end comes, I'll opt for desert loneliness.
I'll require myself to be a wrecked rodeo man
Rolling the ruts in an abused pickup,
Listening to punk and Merle Haggard,
Complaining about nothing.
You'll know me
From the sweat stained Resistol hat
And the coverless *Tao Te Ching* in my pocket.
When it's time,
I'll die in an unplugged trailer house
No one sees or misses
        I want sand on my boots.
        I want no medicine or ventilation.
        I want scorpions on the wall.

I knew a drunk bajo sexto player
Who wiped out on a ranch road
Outside Cotulla,
Catapulted through windshield,
Lifeless on impact.
Coyotes found him two days
Before rescuer sheriffs:
Little remained to cremate.
And so it should be for me.

I praise coyote shit rebirth
Amid South Texas mesquites
Beneath a dusted cathedral sky.
She watches Sandra Bullock on TV.
She forsook every signpost years ago.
I slouch toward naked blood.

SULLY CREEK MOON

She details this cotton-glow spread.
She hoists the sky and presents four quarters.
She is your nocturne and entry.
Whatever is ripe and rising resides here.

You are a ranch boy.
You are an elected buckaroo.
You are your old man's stain.
You are your mother's missing buckle.
You are torn Nocona boots in frozen mud.
You are vanquished spurs.

Hank Williams canters with you.
He rides a four-year-old bay gelding.
He yodels nights so long.
He strums four-four against the waltz.

You've been this way before.

Now the moon holds eye white.
It opens you to the deceit
From lips you pray she never hears.

DAMAGE

In El Paso you scratched time in circles.
You knew cigarette scarred alligators.
You buffed night floors.
Your call extinguished light.

Everyone advocated New Mexico.
But prison passage was clean
As a knife through spring locks.
You begged corn and water

But deposited only air-conditioning.
No one warned you of sand.
Your lungs dissolved in quick dusk,
Unraveling like purple felt.

She pasted her flight in Houston sighs.
You scratched asphalt on her waiver.

LIGHTNIN' AT THE RODEO

I saw Lightnin' at a rodeo in 1969.
I was a scared white boy of thirteen.
Fred Whitfield, who'd become the best roper
        I ever saw swing a piggin' string,
Sat with his family in the bleachers.
He was three years old.
Fred's eyes never blinked. His hands scampered.
My dad was a small-time stock contractor,
A white man from Brenham.
Mother never consorted with the "coloreds"
        — her term, not Dad's—so she was absent.
I spied worlds in the splintery bleachers.
I saw everything good and rich Africa could produce:
Africa, where we all began.
I studied young Fred Whitfield's eyes.
Lightnin' sipped at a Pearl can
And smoked a cigar at the same time,
His own pupils hidden behind yellow-green shades.
As usual, he wore a straw Western hat.
This is a real cowboy story.

Lightnin' loved rodeo. We were at a makeshift arena
Halfway between Hockley and Prairie View
Off Kickapoo Road.
Two black women danced in golden shorts
And Western hats and boots, blouses knotted
      below their breasts,
And Lightnin' looked them over and mumbled
He'd give up a good Gibson guitar to taste that syrup.
I might have offered even more.
Lightnin' picked blues that night for cowboys
In chaps who limped from busted up legs
      while they cursed broncs that threw them.
Accompanying Lightnin' were a man with a washboard
And a man who kept rhythm by dancing
On a pallet cut from green pines that grew along
Big Brazos.
Lightnin' never gave me a glance.
He asked for more Pearl.
I helped Dad load the horses, steers, bulls,
And calves in trailers drawn by two worn-out
Peterbilt cabovers. We hit the big bridge just past
      a midnight that had no stars or moon.
River air swept over my face.
At home, I sang my own blues.

COMMON PRAYER

Dear Sam: I keep the Book of Common Prayer
On a window shelf, an effortless reach—
1928 version, of course. You'd
Appreciate that, I think. Your mother

Dispatched yours with Christian Science
Embrace. I sample a page twice yearly.
It absolves tequila, fucking, and rage.
Or maybe nothing at all. I'm mislaid.

You read your King James with whiskey, cocaine,
And design of pick-up pussy. You held
Reading Room pamphlets inside pillow down,
Your mother smiling agony always.

Let us lift scripture then pray this drunk night:
Two pilgrims riding ninety years too late.

AUSTIN ICE STORM

Rat invasions define news reports.
No attic is secure. Walls are rodent dives.
Three hundred forty-eight arrive each day.
Your yard is a pastiche of spent sour cream cartons
        and coffee grounds.
And why not? Everything else here is rubble.
Even freeway paint declines alignment.
Meanwhile a norther tightens like hipster jeans.
You know what is to follow:
Frozen razors threaten from rooflines.
Fallen lines light up grass in glass cocoons.
Wisconsin émigrés snicker at vacating schools.
Other outliers claim our tires on ice are strychnine.
Maybe they know something. Maybe we should abide.
Lexus, Ford, Mercedes—all abandoned:
Medians convert to auto graveyards.
Even rat invaders fall during these hours.
A sensible man should flee here while time licenses.
But you are beyond serviceable at that level.
You repose below her plasterboard pup tent.
Your storm-shield is her wood and laurel.
You feel her stage her labor and pleasure.
Soon you taste her new coals and broth.
Afterward your rhythm synchs with sleet percussion
        on steam cloud windows.
Hidden rat eyes peer through cracks in other houses.
But you submit. She molds collapse.

GULF VENOM

A hundred feet above the Gulf of Mexico at four forty-five in the morning. I step naked through the sliding glass door and onto the galley. No one should see me. No moon, dawn an hour and a half away. The only lights mark the drilling platforms and channel. She snores behind me. Below on the beach are pickups parked by men from Mexico, who drove up to fish. We talked last night over beer as they fried redfish fresh from the Gulf. They lie in tents now. I feel the heavy damp wind against my body, never imagining that everything here will be storm destroyed in six weeks. I plant myself on the railing, ignoring all caution signs. I don't care. Once I came here to wed. Another time I came here to flee death. Everything repeats itself. I remember she bled that first night. The Gulf surf is the only thing that can cloak the dental drill that never leaves my ears. Tinnitus, the ultimate bad karma. I almost stepped on a four-foot stingray yesterday, in water just beyond the Mexican men's tents. I wasn't naked. The ray was nearly hidden in the sand and took off when my foot splashed down next to its pectoral fin. It shot through the water as fast as a human hurled from a hundred-foot perch. It never attempted to pierce me with its tail. I waded back to shore to return to venom of my own making.

BLUE OVER THE ROCKIES

I.

Tonight she departs, a last whispered exchange.
Tonight she descends to an automobile,
A fluttering of fingers in goodbye.

Tomorrow I'll inhale in the clouds above Denver,
Blue as an old Gram Parsons song, as a discarded
        Gram Parsons t-shirt.
I want Gram Parsons' sad voice now.

II.

I am the only white guy in the complex.
Mota smoke swirls in the legal air.
I am where I belong.

I ponder the trails left behind me:
Dependent footsteps in muddy snow.
I want to see my sister, whom I don't know.

I've never told her a lie. Between us, all is clear.
No explosions. No sinkholes. Just the loss
Of what never occurred, Wyoming bedraggled.

III.

It unhinges me. You drive off toward the Rockies.
I'll bathe myself in those blue clouds tomorrow.
I want you to be satisfied.

I drink tequila for breakfast, swallow the daily dose.
Mind-loss to mud streets and broken pentagram
Years before you blessed me.

IV.

In the name of the Father, Son, and Blessed Pussy
Lost in that level of religion
You evangelized my loss into believing.

It was brush arbor false, televangelist deceit.
Your memory is a vodka bottle.
You hate me for it. Let me anoint you
      in broken shivers.

Another one departs, always another. . .
I'm damned by succeeding.
An old photo, bow tie and braces, lost me.

V.

How to deal with what I inherited?
How to deal with a single tombstone?
How to deal with that Cascades day?
        Ashes of a man I never knew
        Standing against a mountain torrent?

Different mountains, nothing akin
To the rooted Denver. You come by it
Honest, boy, don't fret it. No fretting. . .

I don't know pride.
I know only time.

TEXAS SUPERMARKET PARKING LOT

Inside you weighed alarm and radishes.
The floor exchanged skid marks and spilled
Ketchup as its howdy. You inhaled plastic
Bag restraint. Trapped birds battled
A storm-bowed ceiling. You could not
Ponder fate or faith as feathers fell
On shrink-wrapped paper towel
Renegades, half-price, one day only.
Women hustled rusted carts, fearing
The cereal aisle, knowing daughters
With hate-painted mascara waited.
It echoed overboard: smashed pickle
bottles, naked bread shelves, expired
hamburger. You departed with nobody.

Strange what you never whisper at home.

Now you stand in kind wind.
Sale circulars and leaves flutter.
Asphalt and grackles embrace.
You toe a wad of oxygen tubing
Abandoned at the cart return.
A moon no one sees rises
High against the afternoon sky.

SUDDENLY PONCA CITY

And suddenly, 1987, Ponca City,
  hemorrhage sunsets among the lost,
  Robbie Robertson's album on the Garrard,

You and Bowie, drunk and love-dashed,
  each spool rolled up craps,
  each morning-after only iced grounds,

How did you hand over those women? Fuck it,
  you're two old sports guys, no future,
  just stripped doors and empty bedrooms.

Your hands rest in your hearts, painless,
  and this Robertson album is all gloss,
  and the refined flames are too close.

Bowie tells of when he and his girlfriend stopped
  by the Football King's apartment in Norman
  and the King opened the door blunt naked,

All chiseled sinew and muscle bulge,
  and Bowie's girlfriend had no words to speak
  just eyes wide and second considerations.

She left him that night. You laugh through the tale,
  so boneheaded you miss the departure point,
  too blind to view your own busted turf.

For you, it's just more beer and wallpaper sighs.
  You roll out into refinery refuge
  in a Datsun 280ZX, leaking antifreeze and regret.

LISTENING TO BOXCARS IN WICHITA FALLS

Tonight I huff Joe Ely routing
Butch Hancock's crosstie resonator.
I crave tequila clean.
But a Valley boxer gave me mescal
Sliced with blue hole chill, hard dropping
      my knees.
I stood at that Baptist Church.
I fell at that Church of Christ.
And the song roars on.

No one follows my bleeding.

As a kid I lay awake while freight trains
Howled through a Guthrie midnight.
I knew small things in dead town limits.
I don't shave. My hair's too long.
My guitar's dinged and out of tune.
And boxcars roll.

                    I recall a woman
With eyes the color of Dr Pepper.
She nested a grackle on my head.
She said ache to fly, then vanished at dusk.

The bird took wing. I saw a snake
At the gate, four feet of poisoned gold—
A lazy slither in morning sun, no sleep.
I shot toward the blue, fangs harmless
Against my boot heels, and ran to rails
Silver and tough. The rolling car held me,
My legs draping the open door,
My strings in my lap,
My tabernacle in lost eyes.

She professed Jesus and glass.

LISTENING TO INTOCABLE IN WICHITA FALLS

This dead dusk withholds lightning and wind.
You witness Air Force contrails and fold loss.
You have no idea where you are.
You are every place that gave you breath.
On the wayside, you spy M-B Corral.
You flip cards attempting to decide:
Did Tommy X. Hancock fiddle there?
No matter, it's chained for now.
Still lost, you roll past reconstructed falls:
Today Show/Chamber of Commerce glee.
On to Kemp Avenue and a Church of Christ—
Two Baptist tabernacles and a mini-golf—
Best fast food in West Texas—
Discount dress outlet, blank bank tower—
Forty-nine minutes to Geronimo's grave:
You troll among diesel pickups driven
          by broken roughnecks
And bat an ending of your own.

Three jets more and you hanker sound.
Grupo Intocable lights the mislaid sunset.
Zapata is a slide of 561 miles.
Yet you inhale Falcon Reservoir.
You blossom Ricky Muñoz's accordion.
You become a bleached Resistol, Wrangler's,
          and lizard boots
And dance a step you never retained.

LISTENING TO MERLE HAGGARD IN WICHITA FALLS

You pray to write her a Haggard song:
No yodels but steel guitar.

You want to sing to her about nights.
She knows them: blue light lots,
        airport winds.

You want to pour tears
Into a wobbled microphone.

You offer to absolve yourself in rhinestone.
You need her to embrace the coming dawn,
        unashamed.

She fails closed doors.
She discards kisses.
She declines worlds.

You possess no voice here.

LISTENING TO OTIS TAYLOR IN WICHITA FALLS

She never inhaled this.
She refuted all capture.
Let me walk you now, sweet thing,
Across this loss of needles and blade.
Today just fingers and banjo razors
As I roll through state college decline.
Tonight her eyes flame the feedlot.
I'm told of magician levitations—
        her pupils for deceit majestic—
In this parlor of adjacent foreclosure.

I watch him in 1920s finery.
I lift his blue-steel forty-four.
An Oklahoman oil-rich wedged this door.
I have no words. She repossessed all.

So play this forfeiture, splendid Otis.
I can't cross over again.
I saw another diamondback brown and yellow
Intersecting the foot of the gate,
Four feet of flicker and venom
To offer the strike at no cost.
I squandered her desire and gust.

PART III

MANIFESTATION

SPANISH

A woman once cornered me at a party in the park and said, I heard you were in Oklahoma for a while. I thought that was funny and odd. Yes, I told her. I was there. She mentioned a guy named Link, whom I actually knew. He stole three books of Spanish poetry from me. It was a tilted time. I told her about the stolen Spanish poetry. I'm still pissed about it, I said.

I could read Spanish then, I said. I can't anymore.

She squinted. That's a peculiar thing to say. Very peculiar, she said. She lit a cigarette. I think you can still read Spanish. And talk it. If I could think of something in Spanish to say, I'd say it, just to test you.

I shrugged. Her husband gazed at the monkey bars in the park. He was an Army captain.

¡Esta pobre hombre se va a matar! I said.
That sentence suddenly came to mind.

She said it sounded pretty.

TEQUILA AZUL

I talk to physicians often these days. I never like the advertisements hanging in their offices. I desire no paper preachments of any sort. I am an ethnic Christian by birth. I need the smell of needles and cotton. These doctors parcel me out by square inch of flesh. They detect why I bleed where I'm not supposed to, why my blood pressure thunders, why my kidneys neglect their work. But they puzzle over why my brain demands that I drive, drive, and drive, never going anywhere. Arrival, I say, is failure. Their fingers soar over keyboards and they nod when I explain that Marathon, Texas, is an epic poem, especially in rain. Their heads become rocking horses as I explain that I host an abandoned desert hangar of symptoms and scorpions. They permit a smile flicker to possess their uncolored lips.

Finally, diagnosis: I can no longer process sugar. I must abstain, especially when the sugar is clear liquid in a Mexican *botella*.

I remember an asphalt night outside DFW, July wind beneath her skirt, and I'm eight or nine slugs into a clean fifth of Fortaleza, the fire in my knees and the silk of her neck beneath my fingers. *Pero no más.* Blue emptiness into which I emptied money and love. *No más, no más.* All is cardboard and steel wool in my house now, no sweetness for my dreams.

ROBERT STONE IS DEAD

And on the night ice pellets abseil
These soon to be abandoned bricks,

Rushed news rattles like the frozen rain—
Robert Stone is dead in Key West.

May I be granted absolution once and for all.
I plead for this. I want to you to understand—20 years old

In a building in Edmond, Oklahoma, book absorption easy
As August lightning—

A naked binding sands my fingers raw, *Dog Soldiers* title
As strong as blood, as strong as chrome—

I check it out though Lear weighs against me,
Lear and about fifty other volumes and work and seining for love
(net unwoven, fishless tanks: no hope)

Yet I abandoned all things and drilled my way inward,
Each word applauding each word like, what, Melville?

And then that night of vomiting pain and scrotum
Melon swollen (can I ever fuck again?)

And sweating, yes, iced down shivers
Through endless penicillin entrances
            and Darvon exits,

Pillow propped and struggling with Lear
While *Dog Soldiers* called and called again:

No novel like it.
Damaged for life
Yet functioning

I walked it and read it like a prayer tower call.
You must feel this within me.

And three years later atop granite crowns,
Joe Bruchac, Lance Henson, and I,

We speak of Vietnam, *Dog Soldiers,* and the film,
Nolte perfection, Weld perfection,

And the cloud of buzzards and the C-5 Galaxy slides
Through those naked mountains: It was a time.

Now Robert Stone is dead in Key West.
I cleave my chest for anything.

RUBBER SOUL

What I can tell you is my stepbrothers
Ripped the cellophane in the trailer house
And shrugged it away. Their grandmother gifted
It to them, not me. She passed me nothing.
But I cut my name in green ink above
The Capitol Records dome and staked it—
Forever mine. What I can tell you is
Clamps and crackers collapsed in dim vinyl
The instant the needle stroked those grooves.
I rushed outside and scaled the dying elm
And yanked the locks that had yet to take root.
I knew I'd be bearded someday. What I
Can tell you is that those songs still fly me
Into lost branches of Norwegian wood.
I have survived neon cigarette nights.
I have fallen through hospital mornings.
I have cast burned bone and flesh on mountains.
Still *Rubber Soul* persists
Against my deepening dusk.

UNTAMED CANTE JONDO

She lifted you to the Hacienda Brothers
In Red Bud Trail rain. She bled you thorn and nail.
She laughed enamel bearings. She wept your drum.

Feral parrots once blocked lost Christmas branches.
You cast down hospital venues and teeth iced over.
You knelt in confessional distant to her—

Jesus, holy saboteur! Jesus, who flayed your eyelids!
You forfeit every strength test in that cavern crowd.
The old man owes no repose, nor hallelujah.

He delivers steel with flywheel sparks and spurs.
Yet he never rode a horse or claimed a whole woman.
You know such light. Her beacon wrapped your fall.

This is untamed *cante jondo* with gut strings and maple:
The Hacienda Brothers, accordion nights
In stand-your-ground country, Gaffney's line sublime.

She permitted tears as easy as naked trees.
She owned a Sangre de Cristo thermal embrace.
She gave you the breath of a Taos sunrise.

And the Hacienda Brothers—they resound years
After the first touch of lips in that thunder zone.

SLOW DIAMONDBACK

You slide into living wind again.
That insect night you danced to George Strait
And Grupo Intocable on porch limestone,
So much mescal, so much desire,
Detained too long but breathing now—
And music dies and night declines
            ranchero wattage, embracing
Only the two of you, rising and unbending,
A century oak merged with itself.

The grace you always fancied—
She baptizes you, face and brow,
Then you meld to psalms never recited.

She asks you to fill her again:
End without world, never and never,
Yet you know this is redemption
And you mount her request.
You hold your salvation complete.

You recollect her charcoal hair now
And the slow diamondback at her gate.
You cross yourself in the Episcopal way,
A discarded skin lost in her goodbye.

STATISTICAL DISTRIBUTION

The day you wilted, fire trotted southbound
Through abandoned limestone quarries
Ringed with fishbone and buffalo recall.

A bloodied sun beckons the north now.
I am alone.
I line the skins you shed along fallen wires.
This is the limning of unheeded woe and smoke.

Seas scrub Nebraska, as in epochs hidden.
Shall we be reclaimed as fossils?
No, we are soil that sprouts nothing.
Twenty-first century foam claws....

On the screen women danced out porn.
In the room men reclined with legs removed.
At the door children hoisted bitcoins.
They were accustomed well.

Now I lay me down in realms of ash and saltwater.
Change in the weather, baby, oh yeah yeah yeah.
No other sleek rooms and midnight hums.
Better tune up and sing these blues, old man.
Your time is rust shattered. Harvest you now
Jaws of plastic and sludge but expel nothing.
You are defuncted in evening traffic exhaust.

A SHORT HISTORY OF THE MOVIES

They called him Eagle Eye, mostly. Sometimes Charles Eagle Eye. Sometimes William Eagle Eye. Sometimes just Chief. "A motion-picture Indian, known as Eagle Eye, was taken to the Central Receiving Hospital yesterday, probably dying from a basal skull fracture." *L.A. Times*, January 17, 1927. The day before, the motion-picture Indian showed up at 340 Firmin Street—the house still stands, six plastic trashcans clustered out front in L.A. rain—and quarreled with J.P. Spencer, with whose wife the motion-picture Indian was acquainted. J.P. Spencer laid Eagle Eye out on the cement walk, a question mark of black motion-picture Indian blood oozing downhill. The Grand Jury no-billed Spencer, of course. Spencer's wife bought a new handbag. We are not far from Historic Filipino Town, where boxing matches aplenty were staged at a basement gym at that time. The motion-picture Indian wound up at the county morgue, dead as Fenimore Cooper's syntax.

Thus ended forty-five movie appearances stretched over thirteen years. The motion-picture Indian played Pancho Villa's servant in *The Life of General Villa*. Pancho Villa played himself. Villa called the motion-picture Indian "El Chino."

The General had eyes.

Harry Carr, "The Lancer" of the L.A. Times, fixed everything in four days. At least to his way of thinking. Carr palled around with D.W. Griffith, Cecil B. DeMille, and Mack Sennett. He knew all about bones and holes in the desert. In a column, Carr proclaimed that the slain Eagle Eye was not an Indian at all: ". . .a shame that publishers and movie producers countenance so much loose inaccuracy." Eagle Eye in reality was just a "half-caste Chinaman." Raoul Walsh smiled over his coffee as he read Carr's column that morning. Hollywood was content with itself. Cameras kept on cranking away in waltz time.

STUNT WORK

September 23, 1970, and I sanded time
On a Byrds road crew, last bow to Fillmore East.

> Earlier I straddled gag bikes on *Easy Rider*
> but my film credits are cellophane.
> I had to wash my face nineteen times
> Before McGuinn hired me.

No one fingered his Rickenbacker.
No one could aspire it:
People sweated Humble Pie fever then.
I never followed that septicity.
McGuinn told me about playing Fonda's house.
Gene Clark still flew with the band.
McGuinn said Clark never overcame Missouri.
I told him I rode down from Oklahoma.
I told him I carried a revolver, cheated at cards,
        and recited seventy-six Bible verses.
He hummed "Jesus Is Just Alright."

The Byrds split in Texas.
I hitchhiked to Jemez Springs:
Late September, piñon desire, dark water.
I sold myself as Apache.
The call came one copper dawn.
She bled my knees before I ran.
I doubled Dennis Hopper
Who said New Mexico was stiff
Even as he projected Ranchos.
I felt solid before the camera.
I'd been away too long.

THE DAY BILL LEHMANN DIED

No paved-over grief this bright Sunday:
Bill Lehmann is dying at OU's hospital
And he an OSU Cowboys fan—
That is the summation of all breathing.
No Jack Daniels in the house and you sink
As only botched outlaws can and should.
Just one recourse: *Ride the High Country*.
You watch Randolph Scott and Joel McCrea
As the sky outside brightens in remorse.
You feel like Warren Oates.
You are Warren Oates.
No wise words ever from your lips.
Just misperception and bloodshot flame.
How did you misspend all these years?

Then death-call dispatch.
You forsake all worlds
To silent thunder.
Steve Judd speaks his last.
And what's left for you?

You rise to challenge frozen sunshine.
In ice glare you buy Lucchese boots
You cannot afford. It is your world now,
Drawn up short by your own measure:
No money, no time, walls naked to claim—
Just Goya strings and "Sing Me Back Home."
Bill Lehmann is dead. You can boast no fire.
Uncle Tupelo freeze will descend tonight.
Gil Westrum and Steve Judd hay sleep
As Hammond Brothers trail as the despised.
Your boots feel smooth and smell better.
In shadowland's infected cordial,
You forge a cylinder and carry on.

CAT KILLER

My stepbrother was a small-town cop. He shot people's cats in yards as he made after-midnight rounds. It helped hours pass until he went off duty, and then the serious drinking began. He was a Marine in Vietnam. Occasionally he killed dogs too. Depended on the night. But he hated cats. Now he attends church and flies flags outside his house.

This is the story of modern-day Oklahoma.

Once my half-ass cousin Eddie gave me a six pack of Falstaff. I never understood why he gave it to me. I stored it under Bird Creek bridge on Pine Street. I drank one hot can of beer each afternoon for six straight days. I was eleven. It was enough to give me a slight buzz when I mounted my Schwinn. One Thursday, a speeding cement truck ran a stop sign and nearly took me out as I pedaled. I can't say if I was beer-buzzed that day. Eddie ate a lot of acid over the years. He died at a Salvation Army home. I think he made it to forty but maybe not. He never killed cats.

I weep over each rare glass of tequila I pour these days. I never killed cats either, and I've somehow avoided Salvation Army homes.

WASP KILLER

They arise from mortar fissure,
Mahogany as the bricks themselves.
The searing is ancient—predating
Reptile and bird—the female assault.
You spray your own venom on the crack.
They arise but then totter with wing flick,
Falling dead on Texas summer concrete.

PART IV

TAMAULIPAS EYES

HONDO AND PANIC BUYING

Today I read *Hondo* because I'd never opened any book by Louis L'Amour before, and because I liked John Wayne's hat in the movie version. In fact, John Wayne himself never looked better than he did in 1953, slim and hard and tanned dark as his horse's reins. As if maybe he still played football for USC. John Farrow directed and the color and camera angles were just right and some of it was pretty funny but there is no forgiving the Indian portrayal. L'Amour's book wasn't too horrible. I probably won't read any others.

Today people battle each other over gasoline because of something posted on the venereal disease that is social media. (I relish out-of-date terms no one uses anymore.) Panic buying. A fool was filling metal trashcans at pump three miles from my house.

I have plenty of fuel, enough to drive as far as I want. Maybe I could roll away to a place where no one knows who I am. If anyone asks my name, I'll say Hondo. I'll permit a yellow dog to sleep on my porch.

WE ARE BROTHERS

Just that moment:
Gene and I reel State Highway 33 incarnate,
A morning never born, just night extruded,
Nine a.m. beer in sprung-frame Hornet,
Meadowlark sketched wheat fields,
Downed electric lines, flooded tanks—
        another corpse road crushed—
And Gene is the only steadfast carving.
1975 and why Moody Blues treacle
From the tin tape speakers?
Why not Ray Wylie or Willis Alan or Steve Young?
        Don't spill it to those Oklahoma State women—
        And recollecting her now, these born deaths past,
        Teresa, maybe, or Julia, my head in her blue jean
        Lap as she unties her halter, nipples like
        Vanilla wafers slope to my everything—
        But it's sometimes lonely in our tavern.
Sure, we buck shotguns, we piss in bar ditches,
We roughneck some, we haul hay.
We move a little weed from time to time.
        But it's life deserted....

And we can't speak it.

So we burn menthol. We open more beer.
We discuss song chords and silence.
That is our way. We are brothers.

DECEMBER IN SOUTHERN CALIFORNIA

I.

Morning bled out in San Bernardino:
Slain slayers in a prophet's name,
World without end in body armor...

Later you plow Los Angeles midnight clouds,
Riding the 10 to the 110, wobbling like a GMC
Pickup transmission from forty years past,
Two martinis and wine, exhausted wind:
Buildings like gone volcanoes drink your guts,
No moods left, propelling you to blackness
Perpetual. You recall all your fixes,
Every one of them, shudders between toes
And above the hairline. You denied them
Even as the larva dissolved your face.
How can you unfetter that load?
Thoughts of scoring are bile now.
You have been reclaimed—at least in part.
Yet sweat drops your face at Chavez Ravine.
You crave a dry San Gabriel cavern.

It will be weeks before you grasp
Even this dream is crystalline fraud.

II.

You know his bones
Molder in these valleys:
COLO—STATE—PEN: 18456,
Source of all lost reckoning,
Deposited free in California.

Your grandfather: heroin sire
In braces and a bowtie:
Presbyterian fraud,
Republican angle-forger,
Hard-on drunk,
Lover of Denver storms.

He drowned in dementia spit:
Wadsworth Hospital,
Sawtelle, West L.A.,

Bones gritting deeper.

III.

She speaks to you now:
Her words are moans.
You own her tears.
How can you breathe?
Your craving is lard
Oozing through fingers.
You can't texture it.
And clutching fails.
You nail your face.
You fence your legs.
But nothing retains.
The roadmap reveal
Is mammoth and complex.
You have leagues to rumble.

Linda Vista in rain shadows,
Sand bag crews totaling,
O come ye, hark ye lights,
Nutcrackers tall as Lakers
Guard porch and door—
The Rose Bowl a neon nest
At mountain's foot.

IV.

You paint her loss over Pasadena
Sidewalks as cart people dissolve
In your forfeit. You will align nocturne,
Knifing your valor in car lights,
While San Bernardino hemorrhage
Hardens in desert gentled gusts...

You abide no holy wars or addiction.
Yet you've disavowed your full mirror.
God, ain't you something, cowboy—
You should have shrouded it all along.

You want her, pores on pores,
Time endless. But tonight—
Tonight in this easy topography
You hail only yourself at last.

You do not slay in San Bernardino.
But you're infested with ruin and rot.
Your grandfather destroyed more.
God rest you merry....

V.

Supine on the torture crib,
Guild dreadnought spiked
Above your head, *Fat City*
Papered by the door, wall
Unit heat purr but no sleep.
Pre-dawn jets idle at Hope—
Easy drive, the 134 to the 5
Then exit Hollywood Way.
Check the rental, check the bag,
Check squinted security eyes.
Check San Bernardino slaughter
Updates on the CNN screens.
Check the free drink coupon.

Plug doors alight behind you.
Attendants show emergency exits.
You stand and say:
My name is Stratton.
I am an addict.
I carry genes.
No one yawns.
At ten thousand feet you order
A Bloody Mary for sunrise.

VI.

These things you know:

It is chemistry and gray matter.
It is inward bent shadow.
It is knee failure and vomit.
It is default and repossession.
It is fish scales and monkey feet.
It is fabrication and stacked glasses.
It is words not uttered.
It is too many words.
It is genes and forecast.
It is a room of your own crafting.

A dark parking garage ahead—
There lie your dropped coins
And shrink-wrapped terror,
But she will rescue you from dread.

Yes, she will abide there
In the one sun-warm shaft,
With smiles and eye-glow
To spite all bloodletting
In San Bernardino,
In this cosmos,
In your soul.
Don't affect explanation.
You've found everything.
You dance and yodel in
Showtime spangles:

But you know
Your own lying eye—

VI.

You find nothing inside.
Your paint spatter pupils
Profess diseased hoaxes.
No thorns or steel today.
You only dine at the deceased café.
Your lips drip her marrow.
You photograph the bodies of
      San Bernardino
In skull reflection:
Go West, young woman,
Go West, young man.
This is your welcoming.
In the end, we river-gather
Twenty feet deep in mud
Shuddered by river iron.
My name is Stratton.
I am an addict.
I carry genes. . .
Forever and amen.

CRAZY SNAKE

For me it always comes back to *Zuma*
And a beach mystery I never resolved.
For me it was "Danger Bird" in morning,
Far from California and Malibu,
Just my motorcycle and a dead rumble
Through wasted sand to a Cimarron slough,
Not distant from where Silkwood inhaled her last
Through crushed lungs, her face and smile
          lost paintings.
For me it is that purple dome of stars and moon
And a salt river's deadly autumn hiss,
My bike snapping in a chill breeze predawn.

A woman loved me like a crazy snake.
I discarded her touch for venom fangs.

HAGGARD ON ELECTION DAY WITH FOG AND RAIN

Idiots and broken beer bottles abide.
Her heart is shaved.
Her secret fails ice.
Maybe this scuffle scripts the wind-up.

Her mistakes crook a light gauge.
One word errant and she's misplaced,
Backed to delinquent walls again,
No rides ahead to thaw her.

She hears "Branded Man" on election day,
Rebar bent, concrete collapsed:
Who scores this downward clamber?
She demeans the afternoon touch.

I drop her final glance in fog and rain
To confront rubble and bones.

TRUMPLAND

Mystery jaunt to buy six C-cell batteries:
Next door they jam the Arby's
As Interstate trucks rumble concrete.
You see them, women with walrus bodies
Entrapped in sweatpants and camouflage,
Destroyed men with coverall stoop, beards to belly,
Gimme caps,
Eyes broken to sorrow and oilfield earthquakes.
Status is the mammoth Dodge
And a doublewide with a satellite dish,
The gut-shot buck photo posted online,
Announcement of the nineteenth grandchild.

Here we are in deepest Trumpland.
You move among them, a stranger, yet the same.
You were sculpted by this red clay.
You cannot write poems of politics.
A woman approaches. You knew her
As a cute high school girl but now—
You swallow, you work your gaze—
Now, her face is a wad of bags and rivulets,
Hard breathing erosion. She stocks shelves
At the distressed grocery outlet, she says,
The factory south of town shut down,
Her twenty-eight years there worth nothing.
She has a grandson named Covenant.
Has Jesus blessed you? You cannot answer.
Covenant smears chocolate on his face.

You recall the video your cousin sent:
She is out on the salt plains, firing a Heckler & Koch,
Envy of the family, good job at the state college.
How else to afford such a rifle?

You think about your brother, out on a farm.
The death roll bites deeper into him:
Diabetes, congestive heart disease, glaucoma,
Mass in his lungs, Agent Orange cancer, COPD,
Vietnam nightmares, back shattered by bulldozers
And drilling rigs.
His salvation is Percocet recliners and Fox News.
You have a photo of him fighting oil fire in Iraq.
Now he's a shrinking gray man with forty-seven guns
Stashed around the house, crossbows too.
He raises the Marine Corps flag each dawn.
He expires with whiskey each night, dachshunds licking his feet.
Shall we gather at the river? Dead fish afloat six miles
From his house. Scatter his ashes on his red dirt pasture:
It is the only request he has ever made of you. . .

You retreat in morning, C-cell mission abandoned.
Above you float air base contrails, fading like all desire.
The Arby's lines are bent eels through the doors.

Enough.

You slam yourself into steel, plastic, and leather
And roll away, content with hunger, content to move.

CARTWRIGHT'S MEMORIAL

Again the Texas State Cemetery,
And you are sunglassed and tied
In charcoal and blue, black leather
As always when these calls beckon,
Your best boots caliche stained
And grass jacketed. You opt to stand
In the north breeze shower, no umbrella.
Comanches require no rain gear.
Lipan scalps hang fresh
Beneath your Brooks Brothers jacket.
Caddo boys mind your string of ponies.
They graze among parked BWMs.

Her brown eyes fail a ceremonial scan.
She is gone. She is gone.

Thunder and a puddle grows at your feet:
Rainwater and Lipan blood.
Elders chant tales essential.
A medicine chief smeared by peyote
Sings to a rising vapor bird,
His guitar ancient and battle bashed.
You lived this song.

Later you mount your best paint
And gallop freeways and barbecue lines
Toward clean stones at Palo Duro.

MORIR SOÑANDO

No Chuco Town boy, Valerio Longoria,
Yet as you roll I-10 in sand glisten
He supplies essential pulsation:
Caballo Viejo, more than thirty-years-old
But ideal in this time, even for a fool white boy
In a guayabera, straw Resistol, and jeans.

Her brown eyes peer down at you
From the rearview. You feel her flesh
Emerge through the steering wheel.
In this blessed moment, chump that you are,
You nearly rear-end the cement truck
In the middle lane ahead of you.
But all can be good. You avoid many crashes.
You bottle visage and flesh in green glass
And store them away in a glove compartment.
They will sit secluded for a time
As Valerio trills on.

Later, an L & J Café Madonna speaks Spanish to you.
You pick up every tenth word, maybe.
She appears to be twenty-six. Roses and vines
Sprout on her neck and disappear down her collar,
Then surface on her arms and fingers—El Paso
Tattoos are the best. She is seven months pregnant.
She wears blameless glasses and smiles.
You wish you'd known her for her whole life.
You've never been more at home.

Next you trace the cemetery across the street from L & J.
Chinese stones rise here, as do those of Buffalo Soldiers,
As do forgotten Lipans. You make the Chihuahuan
Trudge toward a cage bent as a house:
Inside is the grave of John Wesley Hardin,
Vilest being ever to emerge from Texas,
And that's saying something.
The steel bars guard his rotted marrow.
You remember Ricardo Leyva Muñoz Ramírez
Sacrificed cats and canaries here
Before Greyhounding it to California
To murder and rape—the Night Stalker.

Enough: You retreat to the rental and return
To Interstate flow. Valerio's fingers
Pursue *Morir Soñando*, and, yes, you could dream die
This evening in walls open to Ciudad Juárez
And farther down the river: Ojinaga, Acuña,
Piedras Negras, Laredo, Brownsville—
Always Brownsville. . .*those eyes.*

You sign in at the Perdió Motel.
You wear desert sand on your boots.
Gray tracks of graveyard dust
Follow you to the stained bedspread.
Morir soñando—perhaps this evening.
You stretch out still clothed, cover
Your face with your hat and wait.
Somewhere beneath a Tamaulipas moon
She is cold, alone, and broken.
You owned her thunder and dread.
Now you own her loss—*morir soñando.*

But no dreams tonight.

Morning boasts clean light and breezes.
You see your lead face mirrored,
And it is beyond abiding:
You possess no pistol, so you fist smash
        the shining before you.
Your image falls in shards and knuckle blood
Onto cracked dresser veneer.
More debts, more scars.
Sam Peckinpah stepped these lines, no matter.
Today it is you who are *persona perdida*.
Even Valerio's music fails you
As hemorrhage smears the rental.
You spread your last tears
In Texas badlands.

THE HEALING

Beef, onion, garlic roar from this cast iron:
Ancient, ugly, grease-blackened, neglected
These thirty years, resurrected this week,
Re-seasoned, blessed, anointed by flamed suet.

You add salt, comino, orégano—
Tablespoons of ground chile colorado,
Thinking back to Arrell Gibson's house,
Gray ice skies outside, bubbling red inside,

Posole in another pot and he stirs
And says capsicum from New Mexico
Dances the tongue, get Apple Valley Fire.
You smile, remembering that chili man.

Just Texas fire today, Dr. Gibson,
But it will do. . .

This is not revolution:
Instead it is cowboy priest liturgy
And healing through hallowed pepper pods.

Palm of sea salt, paprika for color,
A pinch of dried. . .
No, you will share no more.
You fold your best redemption recipe
Knowing you have bested all odds.

Chili simmers a back burner,
Incense holy—
You breathe.
You breathe.

SNOOKER

I.

I screwed up a lot but at least I forsook snooker. That first pool hall was in Oklahoma. In front were old men in khakis at the domino tables. Next came some pool tables. The snooker tables sat in back and had the best light. Which is to say it was dim as a February dusk on the plains even back there.

The pool hall was called the Vencedora because Vencedora had been painted on the front windows back when Coolidge was president. No one ever changed it. As it turns out, the Vencedora was around long before Silent Cal ever stepped into the White House. It had opened not long after the Great Land Run, and many different men had owned it at different times. When Gene and I shot snooker there, a snuff-dipping wraith named Mervin Gray owned it. He'd invested in an RC Cola sign that proclaimed the establishment to be Gray's Recreation. It hung directly above the door. Everyone ignored it. We called it the Vencedora or sometimes the Vence for short.

I wish Merv had swept the tables more often.

II.

Gene and I got better and better. Sometimes we convinced ourselves that we were actually good at snooker. Then the daylight tower (sometimes it's spelled tour but always pronounced tower) crew from a drilling site would come in to the Vence. They cleaned up some in the doghouse on the rig but they still smelled of their job. A guy I knew once described it as the smell of a volcano. I thought that was too simple.

Those guys never messed with pool. They went straight to snooker. They were good. No, they were more than good. They'd win all the money Gene and I had without even concentrating. Then they'd play among themselves and things became really interesting. I saw a couple of fistfights and once a knife appeared. The driller, the boss of the crew, usually stopped the fights, although it was the driller himself who pulled the knife that one night.

Then I started roughnecking myself during the summer to earn enough money to pay college tuition and to live on. I hated being a floor hand. But I didn't want to hang from the derrick either, and that was the next step up. Tool pushers seemed to have it fairly easy, although I saw a driller shove one into the mud pit just before he walked off the job. In those days, you had to put in twenty years to make it to tool pusher. Every tool pusher I knew had an unhealthy taste for I.W. Harper. I couldn't tell that the roughnecking itself did much to improve my snooker game.

III.

I knew I wanted out of the oilfield when I was at college. We called the school "the Tulane of Oklahoma." It was famous for its mortuary science department. There was a good pool hall in the basement of the student union, with three really fine snooker tables in the back. Snooker tables were always in the back at those places. I'd cut classes and spend hours practicing. Sometimes twerps majoring in something like accounting would walk to the back and ask to play me for a little money. I always beat them.

But then this one guy showed up. He stretched his words a little longer than I stretched mine, so I asked him where he was from. That violated pool hall etiquette. It was almost as bad as asking someone his name. But he didn't seem upset. He told me he was a ranch kid from out west of Wichita Falls. Just a ranch kid. Then he cleaned me out, just took two games. He thanked me before he left.

IV.

I had a ten-dollar bill stuck under the floor mat of my pickup. I dug it out and put it in my jean jacket pocket. Then I drove up the highway to the TIT—Travel Inn Tavern—where I bought a Coors and sat down in a plastic chair against a wall. Mostly farmers in overalls and chore jackets were in the TIT. They were clustered around one of those short coin-op pool tables with the wide pockets.

This codger sat down in the plastic chair next to mine. He had a can of Busch Bavarian. He wore an ACCO Feed & Seed gimme cap. Conway Twitty and Loretta Lynn's version of "After the Fire Is Gone" was a big song at the time. Someone had loaded the Wurlitzer with quarters and programmed it to play that song over and over. I was fine with it. It was good music for me to hear.

"I know where you are, son," the codger said over Conway's baritone. "I been there."

"Yeah?" I said.

He looked away at nothing. "Her name was Wanda. Damn, but I wanted to swim her river. Thirty-three years ago now, but I can't quit pondering her."

"I'll be damned."

"You won't get past it. She's poison in your blood now."

I drained my Coors in a hurry as Conway and Loretta sang one more time about love wherever you can find it. It was a true song. "I know you're right," I said to the codger.

"Blood poison," he said, nodding. I understood. I'd been dealing with blood poison since the very beginning.

I crumpled the empty can and walked out the door. I tossed the can into a ditch and climbed into my truck. I never shot snooker again.

www.ingramcontent.com/pod-product-compliance
Lightning Source LLC
Chambersburg PA
CBHW031139090426
42738CB00008B/1159